Coloring Mandalas

Adult Coloring Books
By **coloring.ink**

Artist name: _____

Started on: _____

Use this page to test your color supplies.

Thanks for sharing your coloring experience.

Made in United States
North Haven, CT
04 January 2024

47085001R00076